DISCARDED

Date: 10/17/11

How Do You Measure Weight?

by Heather and
Thomas K. Adamson

CAPSTONE PRESS
a capstone imprint

Ross is carrying groceries into the house. He lifts a sack of oranges and a sack of apples. Apples and oranges are about the same size. And his dad bought four of each.

Why does the sack of oranges feel heavier?

Ross acted like a balance.

He compared which fruit felt heavier.
Using a real balance is another way
to compare. On a balance, the
heavier object dips down.

Ross puts an apple and an orange on the balance. The side holding the orange dips down. The orange is heavier. That's why the sack of oranges felt heavier.

This pepper
is bigger than
the apple.

Which one will be heavier?

The balance dips with the apple. The pepper is lighter than the apple.

An object's size and how heavy it is are not the same.

A balance compares objects.
But people have made standard
units to show an object's weight.

Weight is how heavy something is.

A weight can also be a pre-measured block.

Weight is measured in ounces, pounds, and tons.

    16 ounces = 1 pound
    2,000 pounds = 1 ton

In the metric system, weight is measured in grams, kilograms, and metric tons.

1,000 grams = 1 kilogram
1,000 kilograms = 1 metric ton

In this book, we show the metric weight in parentheses after the other measurements.

Ross can use a balance as a scale.

Scales measure an object's weight.
How much does the apple weigh?

Ross stacks gram weights on one side. He keeps stacking until the balance is even. Small objects are measured in ounces or grams. Big objects are measured in pounds or kilograms.

The apple weighs 5 ounces (142 grams).

Most scales don't need separate weights. Just put the object on the scale and read the number.

This orange weighs 9 ounces (255 g).

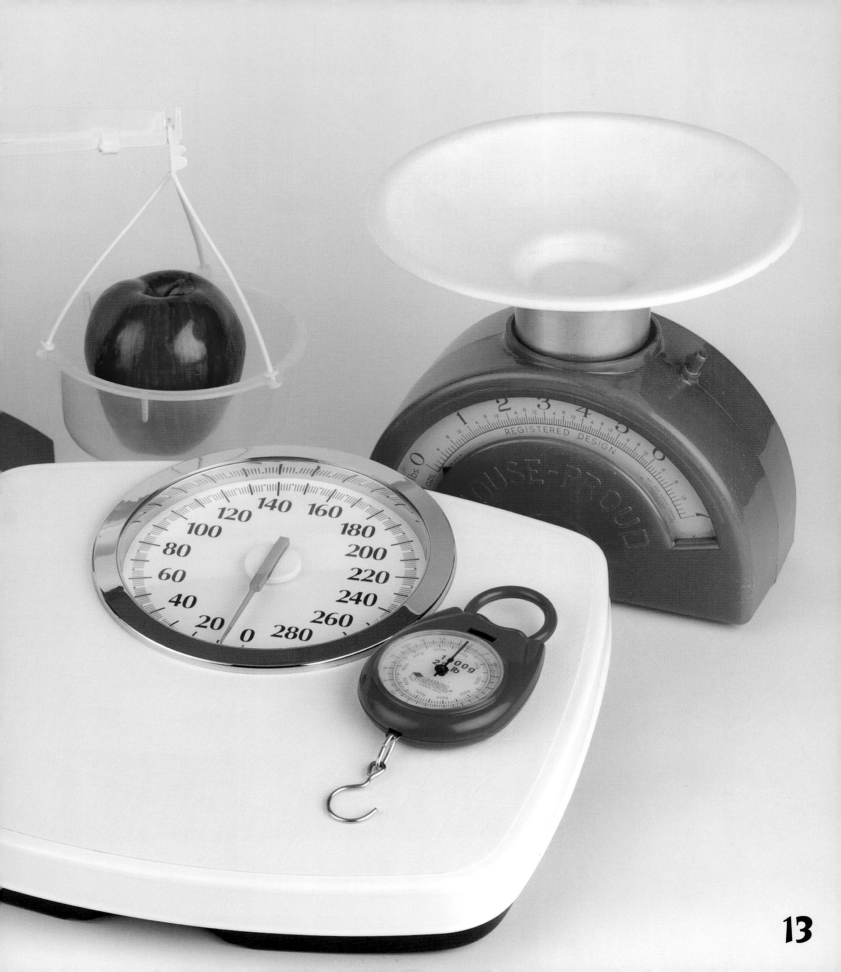

13

Today Ross is back at the store for some candy. The candy is sold by the pound. Are there more mints in a pound or more caramels?

Let's find out!

kilograms

pounds

50kg | 200g
110 lb | X 8oz

Ross puts a handful of mints on the scale. They're not even close to a pound.

Ross adds more mints. **Wow!** It takes 90 mints to make the scale read 1 pound (0.45 kilogram).

It takes only 54 caramels to get to 1 pound.

50 kg
lbs
110
05

50kg X 200g
110 lbs X 8oz

One caramel is heavier than one mint.

Scales aren't just for the grocery store.

You can use food scales on the kitchen counter. A slice of bread weighs 1 ounce (28 g).

Sixteen ounces make 1 pound (454 g, or 0.45 kg). So 16 slices of bread weigh 1 pound.

Some scales are for bigger things. This floor scale at the veterinarian's office weighs animals.

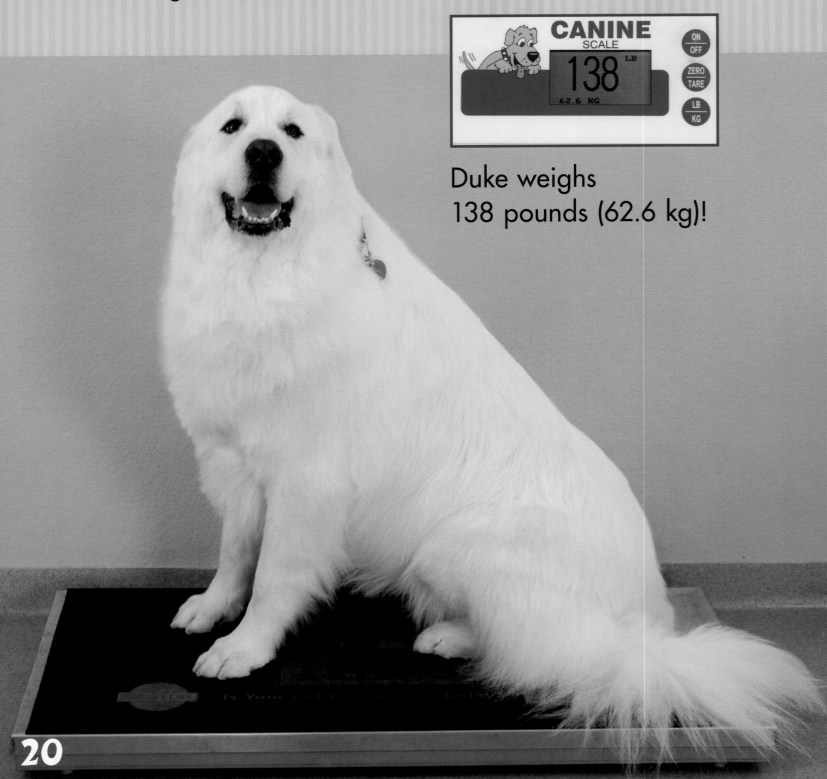

Duke weighs 138 pounds (62.6 kg)!

Princess weighs only
6.4 pounds (2.9 kg).

Some places use very strong floor scales to measure tons. This warehouse is shipping more than 1,000 pounds, or ½ ton (0.45 metric ton) of books.

Grandpa keeps a fish scale in his tackle box.
Ross and his grandpa each caught a fish!
The fish hang from the scale to be weighed.

Whose fish is heavier?

Ross' fish is 8 ounces (227 g).
Grandpa's fish is a little lighter.
His weighs 6 ounces (170 g).

Ross wonders how much he weighs compared to his big catch.

A bathroom scale measures a person's weight. Ross weighs 50 pounds (22.7 kg).

Can you imagine catching a 50-pound fish?

Cool Measuring Facts

a Chihuahua

- The lightest dog on record is a Chihuahua named Dancer. It weighs 1.1 pounds (0.5 kg).

- The world's biggest animal is the blue whale. The biggest one to be measured weighed 198 tons (180 metric tons) and was 97 feet (30 meters) long.

- The largest apple ever found weighed 4 pounds, 1 ounce (1.8 kg). It was picked in Japan.

- The ostrich is the world's heaviest bird. Males weigh up to 287 pounds (130 kg). The bee hummingbird is the world's tiniest bird, weighing .07 ounces (2 g).

- Whale sharks are the biggest and heaviest fish in the world. They usually weigh about 15 tons (14 metric tons), but some may be even heavier.

- Andy Bolton holds the world record for lifting a weight. He lifted a 1,008.6-pound (457.5-kg) barbell from the floor and held it above his knees.

Glossary

balance—a tool used to compare or measure weight; balances have a beam supported in the center with two equal pans on each end

metric system—a system of measurement based on counting by 10s; grams and kilograms are basic units of measuring weight in the metric system

ounce—a unit of weight equal to $\frac{1}{16}$ of a pound

pound—a unit of weight equal to 16 ounces

scale—a tool used to measure weight

ton—a unit of weight equal to 2,000 pounds

Read More

Adamson, Thomas K., and Heather Adamson. *How Do You Measure Length and Distance?* Measure It! Mankato, Minn.: Capstone Press, 2011.

Cleary, Brian P. *On the Scale: A Weighty Tale.* Math Is Categorical. Minneapolis: Millbrook Press, 2008.

Parker, Vic. *How Heavy is Heavy? Comparing Materials.* Measuring and Comparing. Chicago: Heinemann Library, 2011.

Internet Sites

FactHound offers a safe, fun way to find Internet sites related to this book. All of the sites on FactHound have been researched by our staff.

Here's all you do:

Visit *www.facthound.com*

Type in this code: 9781429644587

Index

A+ Books are published by Capstone Press,
151 Good Counsel Drive, P.O. Box 669, Mankato, Minnesota 56002.
www.capstonepub.com

 Books published by Capstone Press are manufactured with paper containing at least 10 percent post-consumer waste.

Library of Congress Cataloging-in-Publication Data
Adamson, Thomas K., 1970–
  How do you measure weight? / by Thomas K. and Heather
Adamson.
    p. cm. — (A+ books. Measure it!)
  Summary: "Simple text and color photographs describe the
units and tools used to measure weight"—Provided by publisher.
  Includes bibliographical references and index.
  ISBN 978-1-4296-4458-7 (library binding)
  ISBN 978-1-4296-6333-5 (paperback)
  1. Weights and measures—Juvenile literature. 2. Units of
measurement—Juvenile literature. I. Adamson, Heather, 1974–
II. Title. III. Series.
  QC90.6.A33 2011
  530.8'1—dc22   2010002784

Credits
Gillia Olson, editor; Juliette Peters, designer; Sarah Schuette,
    photo studio specialist; Marcy Morin, studio scheduler;
    Laura Manthe, production specialist

Photo Credits
All photos by Capstone Studio/Karon Dubke

Note to Parents, Teachers, and Librarians
The Measure It! series uses color photographs and a nonfiction
format to introduce readers to measuring concepts. *How Do
You Measure Weight?* is designed to be read aloud to a
pre-reader, or to be read independently by an early reader.
Images and narrative promote mathematical thinking by
showing that objects and time have measurable properties, that
comparisons such as longer or shorter can be made between
multiple objects and time-spans, and that there are standard
and non-standard units for measuring. The book encourages
further learning by including the following sections: Cool Facts,
Glossary, Read More, Internet Sites, and Index. Early readers
may need assistance using these features.

Printed in the United States of America in North Mankato, Minnesota.
022011   006080R